Information System

SSADM Version 4 Roles

Michael Hill

CCTA
October 1992
LONDON: HMSO

© Crown Copyright 1993

Applications for reproduction should be made to HMSO

First published 1993

ISBN 0 11 330581 8
ISSN 0967-9561

For further information regarding this publication and other CCTA products please contact:

Library
Riverwalk House
157-161 Millbank
London SW1P 4RT

071-217-3331

Contents

Foreword

1	**Introduction**		**1**
	1.1	Purpose	
	1.2	Who should read this volume	
	1.3	Structure of this volume	
	1.4	Assumed knowledge	
	1.5	Coverage of this volume	
2	**Overview**		**3**
	2.1	What is a role?	
	2.2	Management structure	
	2.3	How the information is organised	
	2.4	How to use this information	
3	**Role Descriptions**		**7**
	Stage 1	Investigation of Current Environment	9
	Stage 2	Business Systems Options	25
	Stage 3	Definition of Requirements	43
	Stage 4	Technical System Options	57
	Stage 5	Logical Design	79
	Stage 6	Physical Design	91

Bibliography	**105**
Glossary	**107**
Index	**111**

Foreword

The **Information Systems Engineering Library** provides guidance on carrying out Information Systems Engineering activities. In the IS lifecycle, Information Systems Engineering takes place once the IS strategy has been defined. It is concerned with the development of information systems up to the operational stage, when an information system becomes the responsibility of infrastructure management.

The Information Systems Engineering Library builds on the guidance in the CCTA IS Guides B set: *Systems Development Set* and complements other CCTA products, in particular the IS project management method, PRINCE, and the systems analysis and design method, SSADM.

The Information Systems Engineering Library is of interest to IS providers, helping them to improve the quality and productivity of their IS development work. It is also of interest to business managers, whose business operations depend on having effective IS support by means of Information Systems Engineering activities.

CCTA welcomes customer views on Information Systems Engineering Library publications. Please send your comments to:

Customer Services
Information Systems Engineering Group
Gildengate House
Upper Green Lane
Norwich NR3 1DW

Acknowledgements

The assistance of Michael Smith under contract to CCTA from Model Systems Ltd is gratefully acknowledged.

The assistance of Mrs B Tompkins, Metropolitan Police, Mr I Goodwin, Scottish Office, Mr J Denton, OPCS, and Mr V Zonko, Inland Revenue, is also gratefully acknowledged.

1 Introduction

1.1 Purpose

This volume describes the various roles associated with the execution of a Structured Systems Analysis and Design Method (SSADM) Project.

Each SSADM project is unique with different objectives, level of complexity and scale. However, for each project there is a common set of roles to be assigned to the members of the SSADM team.

The purpose of this volume is to provide a greater understanding of these roles and the skills and experience needed to fulfil them.

1.2 Who should read this volume

This volume should be read by:

- **Project Managers** considering staffing issues

- **Project Boards** reviewing the higher level organisation of the SSADM element of a project

- **Module Managers** preparing for and managing their SSADM Module(s)

- **Team Leaders** assessing the requirements associated with building an SSADM team and any training needs

- **Team Members** reviewing their roles and using the role descriptions as a basis for their job descriptions.

1.3 Structure of this volume

Chapter 2 provides an overview of the SSADM roles and explains how to use the information found in this volume.

Chapter 3 contains the detailed role descriptions organised by SSADM Stages 1 to 6.

1.4 Assumed knowledge

1.4.1 SSADM and PRINCE Readers of this volume should be familiar with SSADM and have an understanding of PRINCE and its terminology. The management issues surrounding the use of SSADM in a PRINCE environment are dealt with in a separate volume *Interfacing SSADM and PRINCE*.

1.4.2 Site Standards This volume is written with the assumption that each role described is aware of any standards, i.e. international, EC, UK or site specific, adopted by their installation and understand how these standards impact upon those roles. For example, the Module Manager may require that a *User Interface Style Guide* is to be followed. As a result, the Team Leader may have to provide guidance to team members on the precise implications for analysis and design.

1.5 Coverage of this volume

1.5.1 SSADM SSADM comprises five Modules; Feasibility, Requirements Analysis, Requirements Specification, Logical Systems Specification and Physical Design. This volume does not explicitly cover Feasibility. Appropriate role descriptions for Feasibility can be developed from those provided for SSADM Stages 1 to 4.

1.5.2 Roles All the SSADM roles, except the User, are described in this volume. This does not mean that the very necessary involvement of the user has been ignored.

The user exists in many guises and roles which depend on the level of involvement, the stage in development, and the type of user - for example end user, manager, budget holder or operator. Explicit references are made throughout the role descriptions to identify and involve the users in the project.

2 Overview

A number of management activities need to be addressed in an SSADM project. These include the planning of resources and the allocation of responsibilities. This volume provides the necessary information to assist in performing these vital management activities.

The important consideration is not how and to whom the responsibilities are allocated, but that each role has been evaluated and defined in the correct project context.

The reader is invited to take the role descriptions presented in this volume and use them in the planned project as appropriate.

2.1 What is a role?

A role is a set of predefined responsibilities. It is assigned according to the needs of the project and the mix of skills available. Individual roles do not necessarily equate to individual people. Several people could be assigned separate elements of a single role or similarly, one person could be assigned to perform several roles.

There are three categories of role in this volume:

- **SSADM management** roles required throughout the SSADM project

- **SSADM team member** roles which will vary during the SSADM project

- **The roles of experts** brought in to advise the SSADM team on matters outside of their normal areas of expertise and knowledge.

There are specific references to the need for experts to supplement the expertise of the project team members in the SSADM reference manuals. These experts may in practice have different titles to those given in this volume.

SSADM Roles

| 2.2 | Management structure |

The following management structure (Figure 1) is assumed for the purposes of this volume. SSADM is used in part of a PRINCE-managed project.

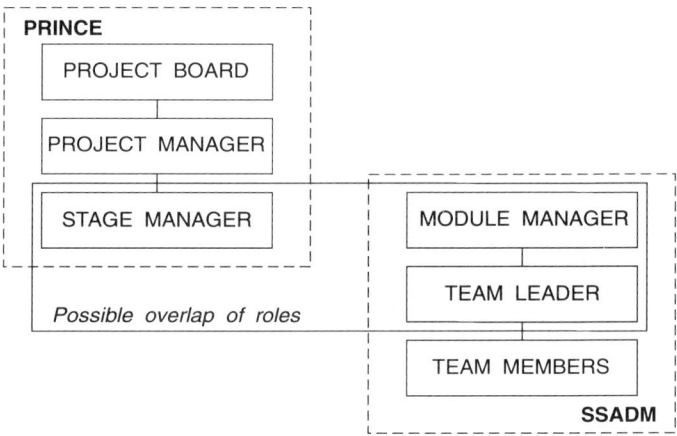

Figure 1: Typical Management Structure

| 2.3 | How the information is organised |

Chapter 3 provides detailed role information. The roles are organised by Stages within Modules.

| 2.3.1 | Matrices |

A number of matrices are provided to present a summary of the information. Each matrix can be viewed from two perspectives:

- the roles required by a particular Stage

- the Stages during which a specific role is required.

The major matrix on page 7 presents all the SSADM roles identified in the SSADM Version 4 Reference Manuals. This matrix shows where each role exists in relation to the SSADM Stages.

Each SSADM Stage is presented with its own matrix which identifies all the roles required within the Stage, e.g. see page 9. It also shows where else that role exists in the project.

Chapter 2
Overview

2.3.2 Role descriptions

For the SSADM managers and team members, the role description comprises four parts:

- **Objectives** - what the role is trying to achieve during the Stage

- **Job Description** - what particular tasks are required to be performed to achieve the objectives set out

- **Skill Profile** - what knowledge and experience are reasonably required of the individual performing the role

- **Training and Development** - what training should be considered in order either to acquire or to maintain the skills required.

There is a separate format for the expert roles which provides advice on what expertise could be required; when and why it is required; and what SSADM knowledge is expected.

2.3.3 Index

The index lists the roles in alphabetical order with page numbers for quick access.

2.4 How to use this information

This volume describes the major roles involved in a typical SSADM development. Further roles may be required in certain circumstances which will depend on the nature of the installation, the IT environment or the system under development. Organisations should tailor the guidance to suit their own circumstances.

2.4.1 Planning a project

Project managers planning the SSADM component of a project should start by referring to the summary matrix on page 7. This identifies the roles required for each SSADM Stage.

The most significant roles for the project manager are those of the Module Manager and the Team Leader. The project manager can utilise the role descriptions to ensure that an appropriately skilled, trained and experienced management team is assembled.

SSADM Roles

In a similar fashion, the Module Manager and the Team Leader(s) can match the project resources available to the requirements identified in the role descriptions for the SSADM team members.

2.4.2 Identifying individual responsibilities

SSADM team members can refer to the relevant Stage matrix, or the Index, to find their assigned role descriptions and use these as a basis for a detailed project job description.

The experts required by the project, from time to time, can be briefed on their role within the context of the SSADM project by using the relevant role descriptions found in this volume.

2.4.3 Identifying training and development needs

Managers with responsibility for training and skills development can be guided by the needs outlined in each role description and matching that against the known capabilities of the individual.

3 Role Descriptions

The following matrix identifies the roles required for each Stage and a page number reference to the detailed description.

SSADM V4 Module SSADM V4 Stage	RA 1	RA 2	RS 3	LS 4	LS 5	PD 6
SSADM Management						
Module Manager	10	26	44	58	80	92
Team Leader	12	28	46	62	82	94
Team Members						
Senior Requirements Analyst	14	30		64		
RA Data Modeller	16	32				
RA Process Modeller	18	34				
RA Product Developer	20	36				
RS Data Modeller			48			
RS Process Modeller			50			
RS Product Developer			52			
LS Process Modeller					84	
LS Product Developer				66	86	
PD Process Modeller				68		97
PD Data Modeller				70		99
PD Product Developer						101
Expert Roles						
Data Administrator	22		54			
IT Service Provider		38		72		
Staff Representative		39		73		
Systems Architect		40		74		
Human Factors Specialist		41		75	88	
Capacity Planner			55	76	89	103
Corporate Security Specialist	23	42	56			
Database Administrator				77		104
Data Communications				78		

SSADM Roles

Stage 1 Investigation of Current Environment

Introduction The Requirements Analysis Module establishes the scope and requirements of the project. The first stage, Investigation of Current Environment, involves a detailed investigation of the current system in order to define the requirements and set the objectives of the new system.

Stage Roles The following matrix shows the roles required in Stage 1 and a page number reference to the detailed description.

SSADM V4 Module SSADM V4 Stage	RA 1	RA 2	RS 3	LS 4	LS 5	PD 6
SSADM Management						
Module Manager	10	26	44	58	80	92
Team Leader	12	28	46	62	82	94
Team Members						
Senior Requirements Analyst	14	30		64		
RA Data Modeller	16	32				
RA Process Modeller	18	34				
RA Product Developer	20	36				
Expert Roles						
Data Administrator	22		54			
Corporate Security Specialist	23	42	56			

Module Manager

Objectives
: To produce and assemble descriptions of the current services, users and new requirements and to deliver these to management for use in Stage 2 - Business System Options.

  To ensure that the products meet the standards set by the installation for quality, content and structure.

  To allocate resources to meet, within budget, the timescale allowed for the completion of the Stage.

Job Description
: Assist the Project Manager in producing the SSADM elements of the project plans. Create project specific Product Descriptions which meet the quality, content and procedural standards of the installation. Produce Activity Descriptions to support product development.

  Produce a set of detailed plans for the Requirements Analysis Module. These plans to incorporate all activities and dependencies necessary to create the products identified in the Product Breakdown Structure and any additional activities required during this Stage. If tailoring the method, then identify those not being produced and obtain proper authorisation. Agree these plans with the Project Manager.

  Agree the Module Plans and analysis scope with the Project Manager and confirm resourcing and timescales.

  Call upon specialist technical/business knowledge whenever necessary to provide assistance in the formulation of decisions.

  Ensure that the standards and procedures adopted are complied with in a manner suitable for the Stage size, timescale, structure and end-user environment.

  Monitor progress and resource utilisation of Stage Teams. Plan for, and handle in a constructive and cost effective way, any exceptional situation that may arise.

Attend progress meetings and produce/present regular reports to the Project Manager in accordance with the project management standards.

Liaise with Project Manager and Team Leader(s) to identify the need for access to Users; obtain authority via Project Manager and User Management; control and monitor user access by Project Team.

Skills Profile

Experience of managing technical staff and delivering significant project products.

Thorough understanding of a product based management method (preferably PRINCE). Sufficient working knowledge of SSADM to be able to estimate effort and plan the Stage within the confines of the Module Plan.

Technical experience to allow full communication with Team Leaders and their teams.

Imagination and skill in staff management, motivation and career development.

Sufficient technical and business skills to take an active part in the policy decisions made during the Stage.

High level analysis skills particularly in information gathering and inter-personal communication.

Training and Development

Training in project management skills. Particular emphasis to be placed on planning, staff selection and financial management.

Broad management and business training in order to establish a better understanding of the organisation and the environment of senior user management.

Monitor new developments in hardware, software, development tools and methods.

Presentation and communication skills training.

Team Leader

Objectives

To assign and supervise the activities required to deliver the products as agreed with the Module Manager.

To ensure that products or sub-products meet the standards set by the Module Manager for quality, content and structure.

To ensure that the activities assigned are completed within the timescale and resource allocation stated in the Stage Plans.

To provide progress and status reports for the Module Manager.

To ensure that appropriate access to Users is identified and authority to contact them is obtained.

Job Description

Produce detailed Team Member work plans for the production of the components assigned by the Module Manager and ensure that the activities and resources allocated are in accordance with the Stage Plans.

Schedule and conduct technical reviews of all assigned products and sub-products.

Schedule and conduct progress meetings with all Team Members and provide progress and exception reports to the Module Manager.

Liaise with other Team Leaders to ensure the consistency and coherence of products across teams. Arrange cross team reviews where necessary.

Advise, guide and assist Team Members in production and use of techniques and standards.

Ensure that the standards, procedures and methods used were determined by the Module Manager. Ensure that all products and sub-products are of adequate standard for submission to a quality review.

Liaise with Module Manager and other Team Leader(s) to identify the need for access to Users; obtain authority via Module Manager and User Management; control and monitor user access by Project Team.

Supervise technical staff and control the delivery of Stage Products.

Skills Profile

Sufficient understanding of the project management methods to plan and control the activities of Team Members under the direction of the Module Manager.

Communication at a knowledgeable level with External Roles, in particular the Data Administrator and the Corporate Security Specialist.

Understanding of IT concepts and practices together with in-depth experience of the techniques and procedures used within SSADM during Requirements Analysis.

Ability to arrange and conduct technical meetings and perform presentations to both technical and user staff.

Ability to identify training needs and provide ad-hoc training to Team Members.

High level analysis skills particularly in information gathering and inter-personal communication.

Training and Development

Training in management skills with emphasis placed on planning and estimating, staff motivation and presentation skills.

Education and training, at an overview level, in the technical specialist roles involved in the development process.

Track the user organisation, its aims and objectives and the systems that implement the business procedures.

Monitor new developments in hardware, software, development tools and methods especially those that affect analysis and design.

Senior Requirements Analyst

Objectives
: To guide the investigation team in the activities associated with information gathering.

  To collect the functional and non-functional requirements for the proposed system which are in sufficient detail for use as a major input to Stage 2.

  To help the Users identify, evaluate and define their requirements within known constraints and scope of the project.

Job Description
: Identify the initial set of requirements by examining the available project initiation documents and define the target users of the system.

  Conduct meetings with the User community; assist in the further specification of those requirements and the formulation of additional requirements.

  Identify current problems and their possible solutions in conjunction with the Users, Process Modellers and Data Modellers.

  Liaise with External Roles and document their requirements and constraints.

  Investigate any conflicting requirements and identify possible solutions.

  Advise and guide the Investigation Team in their analysis and specification of the current environment.

  Liaise with Team Leader(s) and Team Members to identify the need for access to Users; obtain authority via Team Leader.

Skills Profile	In-depth knowledge of SSADM and the wider aspects of systems development.
	Good knowledge of the organisation's systems and structure with particular experience in the business area(s) impacted by the new system.
	High level analysis skills particularly in information gathering and inter-personal communication.
	Knowledge and understanding of human factors as they affect requirements analysis.
	Ability to converse knowledgeably with other technical specialists.
Training and Development	Training in technical leadership and management skills.
	Management and financial training to appreciate the environment of senior user management and assist in developing business cases.
	Monitor new developments in all aspects of IT that impact the systems analysis and design process.
	Presentation and communication skills training.

Requirements Analysis Data Modeller

Objectives   To analyse and gain a good understanding of the data used by the current system.

To document the results of this analysis as a Logical Data Model (LDM) which adheres to the standards set by SSADM and the Data Administrator.

To assist the Senior Requirements Analyst in understanding the data implications of current problems and proposed new requirements.

Job Description   Assist in identifying the scope of the project by producing an Overview Logical Data Structure (LDS) under the supervision of the Team Leader.

Investigate the current system data and extend the Overview LDS. Document the entity and relationship descriptions to produce the Current Environment LDM.

Include all installation and Data Administration standards and procedures when documenting the LDM.

Ensure that the data and processing views are consistent and complete throughout the stage, in conjunction with the Requirements Analysis Process Modeller.

Assist the Senior Requirements Analyst in the identification and investigation of current system problems and proposed new requirements.

Maintain a Data Catalogue documenting each data item/attribute discovered during the investigation of the current system.

Skills Profile	In-depth knowledge and experience of the logical data modelling technique together with sufficient understanding of data flow modelling concepts to validate the LDM against the Data Flow Model (DFM).
	Conversant with Data Dictionary concepts and familiar with any CASE tool designated to document the LDM.
	General analysis skills particularly in interviewing, fact finding and inter-personal communication.
	Ability to converse knowledgeably with other technical specialists.
Training and Development	Training in technical and leadership skills. Emphasis to be placed on relational data analysis, database concepts, software tools and presentation skills to enable progress through future stages of the project.
	Education and training, at an overview level, in the technical specialist roles involved in the development process. Special attention to be paid to Data Administration and Capacity Planning.
	Maintain knowledge of the functions and policies of the organisation.
	Monitor new developments in systems analysis, design tools and methods.
	Presentation and communication skills training.

Requirements Analysis Process Modeller

Objectives
: To analyse and gain a good understanding of the information flows and processes used in the current system. Explore the capabilities of the system from this information, if free from its physical constraints.

  To document the results of this analysis as a DFM which adheres to the standards set by SSADM.

  To assist the Senior Requirements Analyst in understanding the processing implications of current problems and proposed new requirements.

Job Description
: Identify the scope of the project, under the supervision of the Team Leader, by producing a Context Diagram and a Current Physical Data Flow Diagram (DFD) (level 1).

  Investigate and analyse the current system information flows, extend the Current Physical DFD and produce the required number of lower level diagrams. Document the Elementary Processes, External Entities and I/O Descriptions to produce the Current Physical DFM. Update the Data Catalogue.

  Include any Installation and Data Administration standards with regard to naming conventions.

  Ensure that the data and processing views are consistent and complete throughout the stage in conjunction with the Requirements Analysis Process Modeller.

  Assist the Senior Requirements Analyst in the identification and investigation of current system problems and proposed new requirements.

  Convert the Current Physical DFM into a Logical DFM and notify the Senior Requirements Analyst of any effect on current system problems. Review the Data Catalogue.

Skills Profile	In-depth knowledge and experience of the data flow modelling technique, together with sufficient understanding of Data Modelling concepts, to validate the DFM against the LDM.
	Conversant with Data Dictionary concepts and familiar with any CASE tool designated to document the DFM.
	General analysis skills particularly in interviewing, fact finding and inter-personal communication.
	Ability to converse knowledgeably with other technical specialists.
Training and Development	Training in technical and leadership skills. Emphasis to be placed on function definition, dialogue design, entity - event modelling, process specification, software tools and presentation skills enable progress through future stages of the project.
	Education and training, at an overview level, in the technical specialist roles involved in the development process. Special attention to be paid to Data Administration and Capacity Planning.
	Familiarity with the functions and policies of the organisation.
	Monitor new developments in systems analysis, design tools and methods.
	Presentation and communication skills training.

Requirements Analysis Product Developer

Objectives	To assemble the output from activities during the Stage into a cohesive set of end-product documentation, which includes the Current Services Description, Requirements Catalogue and User Catalogue.
	To ensure that the documentation meets the quality criteria and standards set for the project in terms of structure and content.
Job Description	Set up and manage a repository, which adheres to the Configuration Management and Documentation standards adopted for the project, for the products of the Stage.
	Attend technical and quality reviews and ensure that the products meet the required standard prior to insertion into the repository.
	Provide indexing and cross referencing, as necessary, within and across products in the documentation set.
	Assist the Senior Requirements Analyst in building up and maintaining the Requirements Catalogue.
	Produce the overview, summary and supporting documentation necessary to complete the documentation set under the direction of the Module Manager.
	Assemble the final documentation set from the repository for review at the end of the Stage. Update the document set with the results of the review.

Skills Profile	Knowledge and experience of the data flow modelling and data modelling concepts and products.
	Conversant with Data Dictionary concepts and familiar with any CASE tool designated to be used.
	Good skills in technical writing and product production.
	Thorough understanding of the concepts and practices of Configuration Management and document control.
Training and Development	Training in technical and leadership skills with emphasis placed on technical writing and presentation skills.
	Education and training, at an overview level, in the technical specialist roles involved in the development process.
	Training in the concepts and practices of document layout and production with exposure to the facilities offered by Desk Top Publishing (DTP) packages.
	Monitor new developments in systems analysis, design tools and methods.

Data Administrator

Objectives	To provide the project with all possible information regarding the meaning and use of data in the current environment.
	To ensure that all data descriptions and models produced during the Stage meet the standards set for corporate data administration.
	The coordination of the Current Environment LDM with the Departmental/Corporate LDM.
SSADM Knowledge Required	Good working knowledge of the techniques and concepts of logical data modelling.
Services Provided	During Step 110:
	Provide relevant data standards together with any current LDM or sub-set of the Departmental/Corporate LDM.
	During Step 140:
	Assist the Data Modeller in the identification and location of data within the scope of the project.
	During Step 160:
	Compare the results of the data analysis during this Stage with any Departmental/Corporate models and propose adjustments to these or the project's models, if necessary.

Corporate Security Specialist

Objectives	To ensure that the project is aware of the current Corporate Security Standards applying to the project.
	To notify the project of any known shortcomings in the security aspects of the current environment.
	To notify the project of any potential changes to the current standards and to advise on any special requirements due to the type of system being specified.
SSADM Knowledge Required	Working knowledge of the concepts of logical data modelling and data flow modelling.
Services Provided	During Step 110:
	Provide the relevant security standards.
	During Step 140:
	Assist the Data Modeller in the identification of sensitive data which need security criteria applied.
	During Step 160:
	Review the Requirements Catalogue with comments on the likely security implications of certain requirements.

SSADM Roles

Stage 2 Business System Options

Introduction The Business System Options stage allows the management to choose the scope of system functionality and to comment on the planned costs.

Stage Roles The following matrix shows the roles required in Stage 2 and a page number reference to the detailed description.

SSADM V4 Module SSADM V4 Stage	RA 1	RA 2	RS 3	LS 4	LS 5	PD 6
SSADM Management						
Module Manager	10	26	44	58	80	92
Team Leader	12	28	46	62	82	94
Team Members						
Senior Requirements Analyst	14	30		64		
RA Data Modeller	16	32				
RA Process Modeller	18	34				
RA Product Developer	20	36				
Expert Roles						
IT Service Provider		38		72		
Staff Representative		39		73		
Systems Architect		40		74		
Human Factors Specialist		41		75	88	
Corporate Security Specialist	23	42	56			

Module Manager

Objectives	To control the production of a number of Business System Options for presentation to the project board, or designated review body, for discussion and selection.
	To ensure that the decisions made during the selection process are documented to provide a firm basis for the work in Stage 3.
	To ensure that the products meet the standards set by the installation for quality, content and structure.
	To allocate resources in order to meet, within budget, the timescale allowed for the completion of the Stage.
Job Description	Produce detailed plans for Stage 2 which incorporate all activities necessary to create the Business System Options and document the selected system. Agree these plans with the Project Manager. If required, produce outline plans for the Requirements Specification Module.
	Create project specific Product Descriptions which meet the quality, content and structural standards of the installation. Produce Activity Descriptions to support the development of the products.
	Monitor progress and resource utilisation of Stage Teams. Contingency plans for any exceptional situation that may arise. Coordinate the efforts of the development team and users in the formulation and presentation of Business System Options.
	Call upon specialist technical/business knowledge to provide assistance in the formulation of Business System Options.
	Attend progress meetings and produce/present regular reports to the Project Manager in accordance with the project management standards.

Assist the Project Manager to obtain authorisation from the project board to proceed to the next Module. Ensure that the decisions made by the project board and the constraints applied to the project are fully documented.

Skills Profile	Experience of managing technical staff and delivering significant project products.
	Thorough understanding of a product based management method (preferably PRINCE). Sufficient working knowledge of SSADM to be able to estimate effort and plan the Stage within the confines of the Module Plan.
	Technical experience to allow full communication with Team Leaders and their teams.
	Imagination and skill in staff management, motivation and career development.
	Technical and business skills to take an active part in the selection process for Business System Options.
	High level analysis skills particularly in information gathering and inter-personal communication.
Training and Development	Training in project management skills with emphasis placed on planning skills, staff selection and financial management.
	Broad management and business training to establish a better understanding of the organisation and the environment of senior user management.
	Broad overview of the contractual practices of the organisation concerning the acquisition of hardware and software. This should cover the placing of fixed price, time, materials and turnkey developments.
	Monitor new developments in hardware, software, development tools and methods.
	Presentation and communication skills training.

Team Leader

Objectives
: To supervise the production of one or more Business System Options (BSO) as agreed with the Module Manager.

  To ensure that the BSOs produced meet the standards set by the Module Manager for quality, content and structure.

  To ensure that the activities assigned are completed within the timescale and resource allocation stated in the Stage Plans.

  To report progress and status to the Module Manager.

Job Description
: Produce detailed Team Member work plans for the production of one or more BSOs and ensure that the resources allocated are in accordance with the Stage Plans.

  Take part in discussions with other members of the project (in particular the Senior Requirements Analyst) and assist in identifying potential options.

  Attend meetings and presentations with the user community and assist in the identification of the BSOs presented for selection.

  Schedule and conduct reviews of the BSOs produced and ensure that they are consistent with the Requirements Catalogue.

  Schedule and conduct progress meetings with all Team Members and produce/present progress and exception reports to the Module Manager as directed. Advise, guide and assist Team Members in their discussions with users and the formulation of the options being considered.

  Ensure that the standards, procedures and methods used were determined by the Module Manager.

	Supervision of technical staff and control the delivery of Stage Products.
Skills Profile	Sufficient understanding of the project management methods in use to plan and control the activities of Team Members under the direction of the Module Manager.
	Communicate at a knowledgeable level with users and technical specialists and capable of incorporating their observations and requirements into the BSOs under development.
	Good overall understanding of IT concepts and practices together with in-depth experience of the techniques and procedures used within SSADM during Requirements Analysis and Requirements Specification.
	Ability to conduct presentations to both technical and user staff.
	Ability to identify training needs and provide ad-hoc training to Team Members.
	High level analysis skills particularly in information gathering and inter-personal communication.
Training and Development	Training in leadership and management skills with emphasis placed on planning and estimating, quality assurance and presentation skills.
	Progressive education and training, at an overview level, in the technical specialist roles involved in the development process.
	Track the user organisation, its aims and objectives and the systems that implement the business procedures.
	Monitor new developments in IT including hardware, software, development tools and methods. Developments which impact the analysis and design processes to be identified and evaluated.

Senior Requirements Analyst

Objectives	To guide the project in the identification of Skeleton Business System Options.

To ensure all stated user requirements have been addressed and potential solutions identified for agreement during BSO selection.

To help the project team(s) and Users identify, evaluate and define shortlisted BSOs against the users' requirements and known constraints.

To elicit the views of technical specialists and representatives from areas external to the project, whose input is required during the formulation and evaluation of options.

To ensure that the implications of each BSO are known, understood and documented in order that a considered selection can be made.

Job Description — Arrange and preside over initial brain-storming meetings with the project staff and from these meetings agree the menu of skeleton options.

Be project leader in meetings with users and guide them in the evaluation of options under consideration. Call upon technical and non-technical specialists to identify the implications for current services, technical and application architectures and the impact on staff. Ensure that all issues which need to be considered for each option are documented.

Agree to a number of shortlisted options with users and project team and ensure that each option satisfies the minimum requirements set.

	Help the Product Developer produce the shortlisted BSO documentation by providing supporting material, e.g. cost benefit analysis, impact analysis, technical practicability, development timescales etc. Commission this material from personnel internal and external to the project, as necessary.
	Prepare and give presentations to the designated review body and answer any queries that may arise. Provide any additional help that may be required to successfully complete the decision making process.
Skills Profile	In-depth knowledge of SSADM and the wider aspects of systems development.
	Good knowledge of the organisation's systems and structure with particular experience in the business area(s) impacted by the new system.
	High level analysis skills particularly in presentations and inter-personal communication.
	Ability to converse knowledgeably with other technical specialists.
	Good negotiator and capable of guiding a meeting to a consensus.
Training and Development	Training in technical leadership and management.
	Actively seek knowledge of all software and hardware products and solutions that may affect future decisions on system building or enhancement.
	Management and financial training to appreciate the environment of senior user management and assist in developing business cases.
	Monitor new developments in all aspects of IT that impact the systems analysis and design process.
	Presentation and communication skills training.

Requirements Analysis Data Modeller

Objectives	To help in the development of the Business System Options by providing an explanation of the data requirements for each option.
	To identify the implications for data capture and maintenance inherent in the scope and nature of the automated boundary for a given option.
	To document the data requirements for each option as Logical Data Models, if required.
Job Description	Assist the Product Developer to document the data requirements for each option being developed under the supervision of the Team Leader. In particular, record the anticipated data storage volumes and volatility.
	Create a LDM for each option, if directed, and ensure that they are consistent with any Data Flow Models produced.
	Include all installation and Data Administration standards and procedures when documenting the LDM.
	Attend meetings and presentations with the user community as directed by the Team Leader. Assist users in understanding the data implications of options under discussion.
	Produce a LDM for the selected BSO, if required.

Skills Profile	In-depth knowledge and experience of the logical data modelling technique together with sufficient understanding of data flow modelling concepts to be able to ensure consistency between LDMs and DFMs.
	Conversant with Data Dictionary concepts and be familiar with any CASE tool designated to document the LDM.
	General analysis skills and be capable of contributing to brain-storming sessions and user presentations and/or discussions.
	Ability to converse knowledgeably with other technical specialists.
Training and Development	Training in technical and leadership skills. Emphasis to be placed on relational data analysis, database concepts, software tools and presentation skills to enable progress through future stages of the project.
	Education and training, at an overview level, in the technical specialist roles that are involved in the development process. Special attention to be paid to Data Administration and Capacity Planning.
	Build and maintain a knowledge of the functions and policies of the organisation.
	Monitor new developments in systems analysis, design tools and methods.
	Presentation and communication skills training.

Requirements Analysis Process Modeller

Objectives

To help in the development of the Business System Options by providing an explanation of the inputs, outputs and major transformations necessary for each option.

To provide the volumetric information for each option, which estimates the frequency at which processes are executed during peak business periods.

To document the processing for each option as Data Flow Models, if required.

Job Description

Assist the Product Developer to document the interfaces and internal transformations necessary for each option being developed under the supervision of the Team Leader. In particular, define the anticipated transaction volumes and possible modes of operation.

Create a DFM for each option, if required, and ensure that they are consistent with any LDM produced.

Include any installation and Data Administration standards with regard to naming conventions.

Attend meetings and presentations with the user community as directed by the Team Leader. Assist users in understanding the processing implications of options under discussion.

Produce a DFM for the selected BSO, if required.

Skills Profile	In-depth knowledge and experience of the data flow modelling technique together with sufficient understanding of data modelling concepts to be able to ensure consistency between DFMs and LDMs.
	Conversant with Data Dictionary concepts and familiar with any CASE tool designated to document the DFM.
	General analysis skills and be capable of contributing to brain-storming sessions and user presentations and/or discussions.
	Ability to converse knowledgeably with other technical specialists.
Training and Development	Training in technical and leadership skills. Emphasis to be placed on function definition, dialogue design, entity - event modelling, process specification, software tools and presentation skills to enable progress through future stages of the project.
	Education and training, at an overview level, in the technical specialist roles that are involved in the development process. Special attention to be paid to Human Factors and Ergonomics.
	Build and maintain a knowledge of the functions and policies of the organisation.
	Monitor new developments in systems analysis, design tools and methods.
	Presentation and communication skills training.

Requirements Analysis Product Developer

Objectives	To document the Business System Options for submission to the designated review group.
	To document the results of the selection process as the Selected Business System Option.
	To ensure that the documentation meets the quality criteria and standards set for the project in terms of structure and content.
Job Description	Take part in discussions with the project teams and the Senior Requirements Analyst. Document the Skeleton BSOs from their input.
	Attend meetings and presentations with the user community. Document the decisions made regarding BSOs shortlisted for selection.
	Document the BSOs to be presented for selection using information and guidance provided by the project teams, users, Senior Requirements Analyst and technical specialists.
	Provide cross referencing from each BSO to the Requirements and User Catalogues.
	Document the selected BSO and submit for review at the end of the selection process. Update the document with the results of the review.
Skills Profile	Knowledge and experience of data flow modelling and data modelling concepts and products.
	Thorough understanding of the concepts and practices of Configuration Management and document control.
	Ability to converse knowledgeably with other technical specialists.
	Good skills in technical writing and document production.

Training and Development	Training in technical and leadership skills with emphasis placed on configuration management and document control skills.

Progress to further stages in development training in the production and interaction of SSADM end products.

Education and training, at an overview level, in all technical specialist roles involved in the development process.

Training in the concepts and practices of document layout and production with exposure to the facilities offered by Desk Top Publishing (DTP) packages.

Monitor advances in development environments and case tools, particularly libraries and dictionaries.

Presentation and communication skills training.

IT Service Provider

Objectives	To advise the project team on the possible impact of proposed BSOs on existing systems.
SSADM Knowledge Required	Working knowledge of the concepts and objectives of business system options.
Services Provided	During Step 210:
	Assessment of each Skeleton BSO against the existing IT infrastructure.
	During Step 220:
	Advice and amplification of the impact on current systems and services when adopting a particular BSO. During the selection process, give an indication of the likely effects of suggested modifications to a BSO.

Staff Representative

Objectives	To receive advance notification of the possible impact of the new system on staff and their working environment.
	To advise the project team of potential problems that could arise from the proposed changes.
SSADM Knowledge Required	Working knowledge on the concepts and objectives of business system options.
Services Provided	During Step 220:
	Help and assistance in identifying potential staff issues arising from the implementation of a BSO.

Systems Architect

Objectives	To evaluate the proposed BSOs against the Corporate architectural platform and strategies.
	To advise the project team of any hardware, software, network or interface components, implicit in a given BSO, which are not accommodated within the existing strategies. Give an indication of the possibility and likely cost of providing these components.
SSADM Knowledge Required	Working knowledge of the concepts of logical data modelling and data flow modelling.
Services Provided	During Step 210:
	Help and assistance in the identification of non-starter BSO scenarios.
	During Step 220:
	An assessment of the technical feasibility and costs of each shortlisted BSO.

Human Factors Specialist

Objectives
: To advise the project team of the potential impact on staff jobs and working environment.

SSADM Knowledge Required
: A working knowledge of the concepts of the data flow modelling and business system options.

Services Provided
: During Step 210:

  Assistance with understanding the impact of changes in the scope and method of automation on non-automated tasks.

  During Step 220:

  For each shortlisted BSO, give advice on the effect that the new automated boundary may have on the jobs of affected staff. In particular, the relationship to the whole job, variety of pace and skills, individual discretion in work practices and job responsibility.

Corporate Security Specialist

Objectives	To ensure that the project team is aware of any changes to the Corporate Security Standards applying to the project since Stage 1.
	To advise the project team of any special requirements applying to a given BSO.
SSADM Knowledge Required	Working knowledge of the concepts of logical data modelling and data flow modelling
Services Provided	During Step 210:
	The provision of any changes to the relevant security standards.
	During Step 220:
	Help and assistance in identifying potential security risk areas for a given BSO and advice on risk reduction.

Stage 3 Definition of Requirements

Introduction The Requirements Specification Module covers detailed analysis of the requirements for a new system. A Requirement Specification is produced from which the new system is designed and produced.

Products from the selected Business System Option are expanded to include the new requirements. The system data, functions and events are specified in more detail.

Service levels are defined for each requirement and prototyping techniques used to validate the input/output interface requirements.

Stage Roles The following matrix shows the roles required in Stage 3 and a page number reference to the detailed description.

SSADM V4 Module SSADM V4 Stage	RA 1	RA 2	RS 3	LS 4	LS 5	PD 6
SSADM Management						
Module Manager	10	26	44	58	80	92
Team Leader	12	28	46	62	82	94
Team Members						
RS Data Modeller			48			
RS Process Modeller			50			
RS Product Developer			52			
Expert Roles						
Data Administrator	22		54			
Capacity Planner			55	76	89	103
Corporate Security Specialist	23	42	56			

Module Manager

Objectives	To control the production of a Requirements Specification for the selected BSO whose scope, definition of requirements and acceptance criteria enable a Logical System Specification to be developed. Ensure that the Requirements Specification contains sufficient information and criteria for Stage 4 Technical System Options.
	To ensure that the products meet the standards set by the installation for quality, content and structure. To allocate resources to meet, within budget, the timescale allowed for the completion of the Stage.
	To ensure that any specification prototyping is properly managed and controlled.
Job Description	Produce detailed plans for the Requirements Specification Module to incorporate all activities and dependencies necessary to create the products identified in the Product Breakdown Structure and any additional activities required during this Stage. If the method has been tailored, obtain authorisation not to produce a particular product. Agree these plans with the Project Manager. Produce outline plans for the Logical System Specification Module.
	Create Product Descriptions which meet the quality, content and structural standards set for the project. Produce Activity Descriptions to support the development of the products.
	Call upon specialist technical/business knowledge to provide assistance in the formulation of decisions.
	Ensure that the standards and procedures adopted are complied with according to the stage size, timescale, structure and end-user environment.
	Ensure that clear and complete procedures are in place when specification prototyping is used.

	Monitor progress and resource utilisation of Stage Teams. Contingency plans for any exceptional situation that may arise. Attend progress meetings and produce/present regular reports to the Project Manager in accordance with the project management standards.
	Liaise with Project Manager and Team Leader(s) to identify the need for access to Users; obtain authority via Project Manager and User Management; control and monitor user access by Project Team.
Skills Profile	Experience of managing technical staff and delivering major end products. Thorough understanding of a product based management method (preferably PRINCE) and working knowledge of SSADM to estimate effort and plan the Stage within the confines of the Project Plan.
	Technical experience of a general nature to allow full communication with Team Leaders and their teams. Imagination and skill in staff management, motivation and career development.
	Knowledge of the procurement process to ensure that the Requirements Specification is a suitable vehicle on which to base contracts for further development work.
	High level analysis skills particularly in information gathering and inter-personal communication.
Training and Development	Continuing training in project management skills with emphasis on planning skills, staff selection and financial management.
	Broad management and business training to receive an understanding of the organisation and the environment of senior user management.
	Monitor developments in hardware, software, development tools and methods.
	Presentation and communication skills training.

Team Leader

Objectives

To supervise the production of one or more components of the Requirements Specification as agreed with the Module Manager.

To ensure that the products or sub-products meet the standards set by the Module Manager for quality, content and structure.

To ensure that the activities assigned are completed within the timescale and resource allocation stated in the Stage Plans.

To report progress and status to the Module Manager.

Job Description

Produce detailed Team Member work plans for the production of components assigned by the Module Manager and ensure that the activities and resources allocated are in accordance with the Stage Plans.

Schedule and conduct technical reviews of all assigned products and sub-products.

Schedule and conduct progress meetings with all Team Members and produce/present progress and exception reports to the Module Manager as directed.

Liaise with other Team Leaders to ensure the consistency and coherence of products across teams. Arrange cross team reviews where necessary.

Advise, guide and assist Team Members in production and use of techniques and standards.

Ensure that the standards, procedures and methods used were determined by the Module Manager. Ensure that all products and sub-products produced are of adequate standard for submission to a quality review.

Module RS - Requirements Specification
Stage 3 - Definition of Requirements

	Liaise with Module Manager and other Team Leader(s) to identify the need for access to Users; obtain authority via Module Manager and User Management; control and monitor user access.
Skills Profile	Supervision of technical staff and control the delivery of Stage Products.
	Understanding of project management methods in use to plan and control the activities of Team Members under the direction of the Module Manager.
	Understand IT concepts and practices together with in-depth experience of the techniques and procedures used within SSADM during Requirements Specification.
	Ability to conduct technical meetings and deliver presentations to both technical and user staff.
	Ability to identify training needs and provide ad-hoc training to Team Members.
	High level analysis skills in information gathering and inter-personal communication.
Training and Development	Training in management and technical skills. Emphasis placed on planning and estimating, quality assurance and presentation skills to progress through future stages of the project.
	Education and training, at an overview level, in the technical specialist roles involved in the development process.
	Track the user organisation, its aims and objectives and the systems that implement the business procedures.
	Monitor new developments in IT including hardware, software, development tools and methods. Developments which impact the analysis and design processes to be identified and evaluated.

Requirements Specification Data Modeller

Objectives
To adjust, expand and enrich the Current Environment LDM to represent the data requirements of the selected BSO.

To document the LDM to the standards set by SSADM and Data Administration.

To build a comprehensive catalogue of the details related to data items/attributes used in the Required System LDM.

To identify all events that the new system must handle and to document which LDM entities and relationships are affected by any given event.

Job Description
Adjust and extend the LDM to include the data and relationships to support all the requirements agreed at the BSO stage under the supervision of the Team Leader.

Incorporate Installation and Data Administration standards and procedures when documenting the LDM.

Validate and enrich the LDM by applying relational data analysis to the inputs and outputs of selected functions and compare the results with the existing LDM.

Ensure that the Data Administrator is informed of any new data requirements discovered during the stage.

Develop a set of Entity Life Histories (ELHs) for the LDS and then for each event produce an Effect Correspondence Diagram (ECD). Extend the LDM to include new or redefined entities.

Develop an Enquiry Access Path for each enquiry the system must support.

Maintain a Data Catalogue, documenting each data item/attribute discovered during the investigation of the required system.

	Work closely with the Requirements Analysis Process Modeller to ensure that the data and processing views are consistent and complete throughout the stage.
	Liaise with the Team Leader regarding the need for access to Users.
Skills Profile	In-depth knowledge and experience of the logical data modelling and entity - event modelling together with sufficient understanding of data flow modelling concepts to be able to cross-validate the various products from these techniques.
	Proficient in the practice of relational data analysis.
	General analysis skills particularly in interviewing, fact finding and inter-personal communication.
	Conversant with Data Dictionary concepts and with any CASE tool designated to support the logical data modelling and entity - event modelling techniques.
	Ability to converse knowledgeably with other technical specialists.
Training and Development	Training in technical and leadership skills with emphasis placed on database concepts and software tools to enable progress through future stages of the project.
	Presentation and communication skills training.
	Develop familiarity with the functions and policies of the organisation.
	Monitor new developments in systems analysis and design tools and methods.

Requirements Specification Process Modeller

Objectives	To adjust the Requirements Catalogue and create a Required System DFM to reflect the selected BSO. To enhance/adjust the model throughout the stage. To document the Data Flow Model in accordance with the standards set by SSADM.
	To define the functions of the new system and identify those to be supported by on-line dialogues. To define the user roles within the new system and associate them with the functions to support their work.
	To demonstrate important elements of the Requirements Specification to users and to incorporate feedback into the specification.
Job Description	Review the Requirements Catalogue with regard to the Selected Business System Option under the supervision of the Team Leader. Amend to reflect the requirements of the new system.
	Investigate and analyse additional or modified requirements and incorporate the results in the production of the Required System DFM. Adjust the Elementary Process, External Entity and I/O Descriptions as necessary. Define user roles in the new system. Incorporate any installation and Data Administration standards regarding User Roles and naming conventions.
	Work closely with the Requirements Specification Data Modeller to ensure that processing and data views remain consistent and complete throughout the stage.
	Define and document the required system functions for update and enquiry, identify those functions which are to be invoked on-line. For each update function identify the event(s) and enquiries associated with it. Document the service level requirements for each function.

Produce Specification Prototypes for selected dialogues and report formats. Demonstrate these to nominated users and incorporate feedback into the Requirements Specification. Liaise with the Team Leader regarding the need for access to Users.

Skills Profile

In-depth knowledge and experience of data flow modelling and function definition techniques together with sufficient understanding of data modelling concepts to validate the DFM and functions against the LDM.

Familiarity with dialogue design concepts and experience of screen/form design. Conversant with Data Dictionary concepts and familiar with any CASE tool designated to document the DFM, LDM, ELHs and ECDs.

Analysis/design skills in interviewing, technical demonstrations and inter-personal communication.

Ability to converse knowledgeably with other technical specialists.

Skill in specification prototyping and its practical implementation within the development environment available.

Familiarity with entity - event modelling and all Stage 3 products and capable of updating them.

Training and Development

Training in technical and leadership skills. Emphasis placed on dialogue design, process specification and software tools.

Presentation and communication skills training or refresher training. Education and training, at an overview level, in the technical specialist roles that are involved in the development process.

Training on the environment in which Specification Prototyping is to be undertaken. Familiarity with the functions and policies of the organisation.

Monitor new developments in systems analysis and design tools and methods.

Requirements Specification Product Developer

Objectives
: To assemble the output, from activities during the Stage, into a cohesive set of end-product documentation which makes up the Requirements Specification.

  To ensure that documentation meets the quality criteria and standards in terms of structure and content set for the project.

  To receive, control and amend all interim documentation produced during the Stage.

Job Description
: Set up and manage a repository for the products of the Stage which adheres to the Configuration Management and Documentation standards adopted for the project.

  Attend technical and quality reviews. Ensure that products meet the required standard prior to acceptance into the repository.

  Provide indexing and cross referencing within and across products making up the documentation set.

  Assist the Team Leaders and Team Members to maintain the Requirements Catalogue.

  Produce the overview, summary and supporting documentation necessary to complete the documentation set under the direction of the Module Manager.

  Assemble the final documentation set from the repository for review at the end of the Stage. Update the document set with the results of the review.

Skills Profile	Knowledge and experience of the data flow modelling, logical data modelling, entity - event modelling, dialogue design and function definition techniques.
	Conversant with Data Dictionary concepts and familiar with any CASE tool or Desk Top Publishing (DTP) package designated to be used on the project.
	Thorough understanding of the concepts and practices of Configuration Management and Document Control.
	Good skills in technical writing and document production.
Training and Development	Training in technical and leadership skills with emphasis placed on technical writing and presentation skills.
	Education and training, at an overview level, in the technical specialist roles that are involved in the development process.
	Training in the concepts and practices of document layout and production with exposure to the facilities offered by various Desk Top Publishing (DTP) packages.
	Monitor new developments in systems analysis and design tools and methods.

Data Administrator

Objectives	To provide the project with all possible information regarding the meaning and use of data within the scope of the project.
	To ensure that all data descriptions and models produced during the Stage meet the standards set for corporate data administration.
	The coordination of the Required System LDM with the Departmental/Corporate LDM.
SSADM Knowledge Required	Good working knowledge of the techniques and concepts of logical data modelling and relational data analysis.
Services Provided	During Step 320:
	The provision of the relevant data standards together with any sub-set of the Departmental/Corporate LDM.
	During Step 340:
	To compare the results of the data analysis during this Stage with any Corporate/Departmental models and to propose adjustments to these or the project models.

Capacity Planner

Objectives
: To assist the Requirements Specification Process Modeller in identifying potential problems in meeting the service level requirements set for each function.

  To receive advance notification of the capacity requirements of the new system.

SSADM Knowledge Required
: Working knowledge of the concepts of function definition and requirements definition and their implications for capacity planning.

Services Provided
: During Step 330:

  Advice and guidance to the Requirements Specification Process Modeller in defining the service level requirements for each function.

  During Step 370:

  A review of the Requirements Catalogue and Function Catalogue.

Corporate Security Specialist

Objectives	To assist the Requirements Specification Data Modeller in identifying entities, attributes and relationships which are required for the non-functional aspects of security and access control.
	To ensure that all the requirements of Corporate Security are documented in the Requirements Catalogue.
SSADM Knowledge Required	Working knowledge of the concepts of logical data modelling, data flow modelling and requirements definition and how they relate to the Requirements Catalogue.
Services Provided	During Step 320:
	Advice and guidance to the Data Modeller in modelling the data requirements relating to security.
	During Step 340:
	Help and assist in identifying potential security risks as a result of the identification of system functions and their mode of operation.
	During Step 370:
	Review the security requirements in the Requirements Catalogue and their incorporation into the appropriate products of the Requirements Specification.

Stage 4 Technical System Options

Introduction The Logical System Specification Module comprises two streams of activity covering the technical environment (Technical System Options) for implementation and the design for the implementation (Logical Design).

Technical System Options provide for the selection of technical environment from a range of options.

Stage Roles The following matrix shows the roles required in Stage 4 and a page number reference to the detailed description.

SSADM V4 Module SSADM V4 Stage	RA 1	RA 2	RS 3	LS 4	LS 5	PD 6
SSADM Management						
Module Manager	10	26	44	58	80	92
Team Leader	12	28	46	62	82	94
Team Members						
Senior Requirements Analyst	14	30		64		
LS Product Developer				66	86	
PD Process Modeller				68		97
PD Data Modeller				70		99
Expert Roles						
IT Service Provider		38		72		
Staff Representative		39		73		
Systems Architect		40		74		
Human Factors Specialist		41		75	88	
Capacity Planner			55	76	89	103
Database Administrator				77		104
Data Communications				78		

Module Manager

Objectives	To control the production of a number of Technical System Options (TSO) to enable management to select the technical environment which represents the best value in meeting the requirements of the new system.
	To ensure that all TSOs have been subjected to capacity planning assessment.
	To ensure that selection process results are documented in a consolidated Technical Environment Description supported by an Application Style Guide.
	To ensure that the products meet the standards set by the installation for quality, content and structure.
	To allocate resources to meet, within budget, the timescale allowed for the completion of the Stage.
	To ensure that the TSOs comply with current organisational practices for procurement and management.
Job Description	Produce detailed plans for this Module to incorporate all activities and dependencies necessary to create the products identified in the Product Breakdown Structure and any additional activities required during this Stage. If the method has been tailored, obtain authorisation not to produce a particular product. Agree these plans with the Project Manager.
	Produce outline plans for the Physical Design Module.
	Create Product Descriptions which meet installation quality, content and structural standards. Produce Activity Descriptions to support development of the products.
	Coordinate the efforts of the TSO group and users in the formulation and production of the options submitted for selection.

Call upon specialist technical/business knowledge to provide input to the formulation of TSOs.

Produce an Outline Development Plan for the remainder of the development for each option submitted.

Finalise the TSOs and present them to the project board identifying the strengths and weaknesses of each option.

Supervise the consolidation of the results of the selection process into the end stage products.

Ensure that the standards and procedures adopted are complied with according to the system complexity, timescale, any predefined IT platform and adopted procurement strategies.

Monitor progress and resource utilisation of Stage Teams. Contingency plans for any exceptional situation that may arise.

Attend progress meetings and produce/present regular reports to the Project Manager in accordance with the project management standards.

Skills Profile	Experience of managing technical staff and delivering significant project products.
	Thorough understanding of a product based management method (preferably PRINCE) and sufficient working knowledge of SSADM to estimate effort and plan the Stage within the confines of the Module Plan.
	General technical experience to allow full communication with Team Leaders, their teams and technical specialists.
	Management and control of external contractors if a technical design study is undertaken by contracted organisations.
	Imagination and skill in staff management, motivation and career development.
	Technical and business skills to take an active part in the policy decisions made during the Stage.
	High level analysis skills particularly in information gathering and inter-personal communication.
Training and Development	Continuing training in project management with emphasis placed on planning skills, staff selection and financial management.
	Broad management and business training to establish a better understanding of the organisation and the environment of senior user management.
	Broad overview of the contractual practices of the organisation in relation to the acquisition of hardware and software. This should cover the placing of fixed price, time and materials and turnkey developments.
	Monitor new developments in hardware, software, development tools and methods.
	Presentation and communication skills training.

Team Leader

Objectives
: To supervise the production of one or more TSOs as agreed with the Module Manager.

  To ensure that the TSOs meet the standards set by the Module Manager for quality, content and structure.

  To ensure that the activities assigned are completed within the timescale and resource allocation in the Stage Plans.

  To report progress and status to the Module Manager.

Job Description
: Produce detailed Team Member work plans for the production of the components assigned by the Module Manager and ensure that the activities and resources allocated are in accordance with the Stage Plans.

  Take part in discussions with other members of the TSO group and users to assist in identifying potential options. Attend meetings and presentations and assist in the identification of TSOs to be presented for selection.

  Schedule and conduct technical reviews of all assigned products and sub-products.

  Schedule and conduct progress meetings with all Team Members and produce/present progress and exception reports to the Module Manager as directed.

  Liaise with other Team Leaders to ensure the consistency and coherence of products across teams. Arrange cross team reviews where necessary.

  Advise, guide and assist Team Members in production and use of techniques and standards.

  Ensure that the standards, procedures and methods used were determined by the Module Manager. Ensure that all products and sub-products produced are of adequate standard for submission to a quality review.

Skills Profile	Supervision of technical staff and control the delivery of Stage Products.
	Understanding of project management methods in use to plan and control the activities of Team Members as directed by the Module Manager.
	Communicate at a knowledgeable level with Technical Specialists.
	Understand IT concepts and practices together with in-depth experience of the techniques and procedures used during Technical System Options.
	Ability to conduct technical meetings and deliver presentations to both technical and user staff.
	Ability to identify training needs and to provide ad-hoc training to Team Members.
	High level analysis skills particularly in information gathering and inter-personal communication.
Training and Development	Training in management skills with emphasis placed on planning and estimating, staff motivation and presentation skills.
	Education and training, at an overview level, in the technical specialist roles involved in the development process.
	Track the user organisation, its aims and objectives and the systems that implement the business procedures.
	Monitor new developments in IT including hardware, software, development tools and methods. Developments which impact the analysis and design processes to be identified and evaluated.

Senior Requirements Analyst

Objectives
: To ensure that all Technical System Options considered satisfy the base constraints imposed on the development.

  To evaluate each technical environment proposed against the service level requirements contained in the Requirements Specification.

  To help Users in the evaluation and selection of a technical environment from the options presented.

  To obtain all relevant information from supply sources regarding the products/services considered as candidates for inclusion in TSOs.

Job Description
: Identify the constraints contained within the project documentation and relevant strategy documents and record these as the base constraints for the TSOs.

  Conduct meetings with the TSO group/users and assist in the production of a shortlist of options.

  Produce a System Description for each shortlisted option, which states how the system satisfies the requirements and indicate any requirements that the option fails to satisfy.

  Validate the options against the service level requirements for each function and highlight any variances found.

  Produce a cost/benefit analysis and impact analysis for each TSO presented.

  Assist the Module Manager in presenting the TSOs to the user management and provide advice and guidance in understanding the implications of the options.

Skills Profile	In-depth knowledge of SSADM and the wider aspects of systems development.
	Knowledge of the organisations systems and structure with experience in the business area(s) impacted by the new system.
	Display high level analysis skills in presentation techniques, cost/benefit analysis, impact analysis and inter-personal communication.
	Ability to converse knowledgeably with other technical specialists.
Training and Development	Training in technical leadership and management skills.
	Actively seek knowledge of all software and hardware products and solutions that may affect future decisions on system building or enhancement.
	Management and financial training to appreciate the environment of senior user management and assist in developing business cases.
	Monitor new developments in all aspects of IT that impact the systems analysis and design process.
	Presentation and communication skills training.

Logical Specification Product Developer

Objectives	To document the Technical System Options submitted to the project board for selection.

To document the results of the selection process as the Selected TSO and its Technical Environment Description.

To ensure that the documentation meets the quality criteria and standards in terms of structure and content set for the project. |
| Job Description | Take part in discussions with the TSO group/users and document the Skeleton TSOs from their input.

Attend meetings and presentations with the TSO group/user community and document the decisions made regarding TSOs shortlisted for selection.

Document the TSOs to be presented for selection using information and guidance provided by the Module Manager, TSO group, Senior Requirements Analyst and technical specialists.

Rework elements of the selected TSO to reflect the decisions taken at the end of the selection process.

Assemble the Technical Environment Description from information and documentation supplied by the TSO group and technical specialists.

Produce the Application Style Guide from the results of the Specification Prototyping exercise and the existing installation standard style guide. Produce the guide with the help and assistance of the Human Factors Specialists.

Submit the Stage end products for review. Ensure that the documents are reworked with the results of the review. |

Skills Profile	Knowledge and experience of all the SSADM techniques and concepts through to the end of Stage 4 together with an understanding of dialogue and form design.
	Thorough understanding of the concepts and practices of Configuration Management and document control.
	Ability to communicate with other technical specialists and produce documentation which reflects the advice given.
	Good skills in technical writing and document production.
Training and Development	Training in technical and leadership skills with emphasis placed on configuration management and document control skills.
	Education and training, at an overview level, in all technical specialist roles involved in the development process.
	Training in the concepts and practices of document layout and production with exposure to the facilities offered by Desk Top Publishing (DTP) packages.
	Monitor advances in development environments and case tools, particularly libraries and dictionaries.
	Presentation and communication skills training.

Physical Design Process Modeller

Objectives	To assist in the production of the Technical System Options by providing process volumetric and sizing information for each option presented.
	To ensure that human factors are considered when the TSOs are being proposed.
Job Description	Produce estimates of the transaction volumes and physical program/module sizes across the application architecture of each proposed option under the supervision of the Team Leader.
	Include all programming and physical environment specific standards/requirements when producing the estimates.
	Ensure that processing and data views are consistent across TSOs in conjunction with the Physical Design Data Modeller.
	Ensure that the user environment aspects and characteristics are consistent across TSOs in conjunction with the Human Factors Specialist.
Skills Profile	Knowledge and experience of the function definition and physical process specification techniques together with experience of the hardware and software characteristics of each technical environment.
	Ability to converse knowledgeably with other technical specialists.

| Training and Development | Training in technical and leadership skills. |

Education and training, at an overview level, in the technical specialist roles involved in the development process. Special attention to be paid to Human Factors, Ergonomics, Database Administration and Capacity Planning.

Specific training in the concepts and use of products which make up the technical architectures within the organisation. This to include databases, application generators, software utilities, local and wide area networks and system management tools.

Understand the functions and policies of the organisation.

Monitor new developments in systems analysis and design tools and methods.

Presentation and communication skills training.

Physical Design Data Modeller

Objectives
: To assist in the production of the Technical System Options by providing data volumetric and sizing information for each option presented.

Job Description
: Produce estimates of the data volumes and physical data set sizes across the application architecture of each proposed option under the supervision of the Team Leader.

  Take into account all Data Administration, Database Administration and physical environment specific standards/requirements when producing estimates.

  Ensure that data and processing views are consistent across TSOs in conjunction with the Physical Design Process Modeller.

Skills Profile
: Knowledge and experience of the logical data modelling and physical data design techniques together with an understanding of the hardware and software characteristics of each technical environment.

  Ability to converse knowledgeably with other technical specialists.

Training and Development

Training in technical and leadership skills.

Education and training, at an overview level, in the technical specialist roles involved in the development process. Special attention to be paid to Database Administration and Capacity Planning.

Specific training in the concepts and use of products which make up the technical architectures within the organisation. This to include databases, application generators, software utilities, local and wide area networks and system management tools.

Understand the functions and policies of the organisation.

Monitor new developments in systems analysis and design tools and methods.

Presentation and communication skills training.

IT Service Provider

Objectives	To advise the TSO group of the impact of each proposed TSO on existing systems.
SSADM Knowledge Required	Working knowledge of the concepts and objectives of Technical System Option production.
Services Provided	During Step 410:
	Assessment of each Skeleton TSO against the existing systems and services.
	During Step 420:
	Impact analysis of the effects on current systems and services of adopting a particular TSO.
	During the selection process, give an indication of the likely effects of suggested modifications to a TSO.

Staff Representative

Objectives	To advise the TSO group of the possible impact of each proposed TSO on staff and their working environment.
	To provide input to the Impact Analysis regarding the implications for staff resulting from the selection of a TSO.
SSADM Knowledge Required	Working knowledge of the concepts and objectives of Technical System Option production.
Services Provided	During Step 410:
	Help and assistance in the identification of changes to the staffing levels, staff distribution and operating procedures if a given TSO is selected.
	During Step 420:
	Assessment of the impact the chosen option has on staff together with recommendations regarding the training, methods and procedures to be adopted to ease the transition to the new system.

Systems Architect

Objectives

To evaluate the proposed TSOs against the Corporate systems architecture and strategies.

To advise the TSO group of any hardware, software or system interface components required for a given TSO which are not accommodated within the existing strategies and give an indication of the possibility of providing these components.

SSADM Knowledge Required

Working knowledge of the concepts of logical data modelling and data flow modelling and I/O Descriptions.

Services Provided

During Step 410:

Help and assistance in the identification of non-starter TSO scenarios.

During Step 420:

Assessment of the technical feasibility and fit of each proposed TSO with the current systems architecture and strategies. Provide advice on the effects of decisions made during the selection process.

Human Factors Specialist

Objectives
: To provide the TSO group with an evaluation of each TSO, identifying the effect on the physical working environment of the user.

  To provide an assessment of the suitability of hardware interface mechanisms in the TSOs against the type and operating mode of each man/machine interface in the new system.

SSADM Knowledge Required
: Working knowledge of the concepts and objectives of Technical System Option production.

Services Provided
: During Step 410:

  Assessment of the needs of users for particular hardware and environmental characteristics. This includes legal requirements for Health and Safety; any EC regulations, e.g. EC Directive 90/270/EEC on VDUs; organisational standards; ergonomic issues; job needs and staff Human Computer Interface needs.

Capacity Planner

Objectives	To assist in the evaluation of the proposed TSOs and advise on their suitability in supporting the Requirements Specification.
	To advise the TSO group of the practicability of the desired Service Level Requirements.
SSADM Knowledge Required	Working knowledge of the concepts of logical data modelling, data flow modelling and I/O Descriptions.
Services Provided	During Step 410:
	Help and assistance in the identification of non-starter TSO scenarios. Receive and evaluate Capacity Planning Input and pass the results back to the TSO group.
	During Step 420:
	Assessment of the technical feasibility of each proposed TSO based on the results of Capacity Workload Modelling. Validation of the Service Level Requirements for the chosen TSO together with an evaluation of the design objectives set for the system.

Database Administrator

Objectives	To advise the TSO group of the capabilities, advantages and disadvantages of DBMS and File Handlers under consideration.
	To provide an assessment of the impact of the chosen option on current database facilities.
SSADM Knowledge Required	Working knowledge of the concepts of function definition and logical data modelling.
Services Provided	During Step 410:
	Assistance with understanding the realistic performance expected from various proprietary data storage and retrieval mechanisms.
	During Step 420:
	Assessment of the suitability of the currently installed DBMS/File Handler facilities for the proposed options with advice on additional facilities which may be needed to augment/replace current facilities.

Data Communications

Objectives	To evaluate the proposed TSOs against the Corporate network and communications architecture and strategies.
	To advise the TSO group of any network or interface facilities required by a given TSO which are not accommodated within the existing architecture and strategies.
SSADM Knowledge Required	Working knowledge of the concepts of logical data modelling, data flow modelling and an understanding of function definition.
Services Provided	During Step 420:
	Assessment of the technical feasibility and fit of each proposed TSO with the current network and communications architecture and strategies. Advice regarding the capabilities of the current architecture to cope with the expected volumes, throughput and recovery requirements of the proposed TSOs.

Stage 5 Logical Design

Introduction The second stage, Logical Design, of the Logical System Specification Module details the components of the Requirements Specification to provide an implementation level specification.

Stage Roles The following matrix shows the roles required in Stage 5 and a page number reference to the detailed description.

SSADM V4 Module / SSADM V4 Stage	RA 1	RA 2	RS 3	LS 4	LS 5	PD 6
SSADM Management						
Module Manager	10	26	44	58	80	92
Team Leader	12	28	46	62	82	94
Team Members						
LS Process Modeller					84	
LS Product Developer				66	86	
Expert Roles						
Human Factors Specialist		41		75	88	
Capacity Planner			55	76	89	103

Module Manager

Objectives	To control the production and assembly of a Logical Design which is non-procedural and can be implemented on a range of technical platforms.
	To ensure that the Logical Design produced satisfies all requirements stated in the Requirements Specification including any modifications found to be necessary during Technical System Options.
	To ensure that the products produced meet the standards set by the installation for quality, content and structure.
	To allocate resources to meet, within budget, the timescale allowed for the completion of the Stage.
Job Description	Produce detailed plans for this Module which incorporate all activities and dependencies necessary to create the products identified in the Product Breakdown Structure plus any additional activities required during this Stage. If the method has been tailored, obtain authorisation not to produce a particular product. Agree these plans with the Project Manager.
	Produce outline plans for the Physical Design Module.
	Create Product Descriptions which meet the quality, content and structural standards set for the project. Produce Activity Descriptions to support the development of the products.
	Call upon specialist technical/business knowledge whenever necessary to provide assistance in the formulation of decisions.
	Ensure that the standards and procedures adopted are complied with according to stage size, timescale, structure and end-user environment.
	Monitor progress and resource utilisation of Stage Teams. Contingency plans for any exceptional situation that may arise.

	Attend progress meetings and produce/present regular reports to the Project Manager in accordance with the project management standards.
	Liaise with Project Manager and Team Leader(s) to identify the need for access to Users; obtain authority via Project Manager and User Management; control and monitor user access by Project Team.
Skills Profile	Experience of managing technical staff and delivering major end products.
	Thorough understanding of a product based management method (preferably PRINCE) and sufficient working knowledge of SSADM to estimate effort and plan the Stage within the confines of the Project Plan.
	Technical experience of a general nature to allow full communication with Team Leaders and their teams.
	Imagination and skill in staff management, motivation and career development.
	High level analysis skills particularly in information gathering and inter-personal communication.
Training and Development	Continuing training in project management with emphasis placed on planning skills, staff selection and financial management.
	Broad management and business training to establish a better understanding of the organisation, and the environment of senior user management.
	Monitor new developments in hardware, software, development tools and methods.
	Presentation and communication skills training.

Team Leader

Objectives

To supervise the production of one or more components of the Logical Design as agreed with the Module Manager.

To ensure that the products or sub-products produced meet the standards set by the Module Manager for quality, content and structure.

To ensure that the activities assigned are completed within the timescale and resource allocation stated in the Stage Plans.

To report progress and status to the Module Manager.

Job Description

Produce detailed Team Member work plans for the production of the components assigned by the Module Manager and ensure that the activities and resources allocated are in accordance with the Stage Plans.

Schedule and conduct technical reviews of all assigned products and sub-products.

Schedule and conduct progress meetings with all Team Members and produce/present progress and exception reports to the Module Manager as directed.

Liaise with other Team Leaders to ensure the consistency and coherence of products across teams. Arrange cross team reviews where necessary.

Advise, guide and assist Team Members in production and the use of techniques and standards.

Ensure that the standards, procedures and methods used were determined by the Module Manager. Also ensure that all products and sub-products are of adequate standard for submission to a quality review.

	Liaise with Module Manager and Team Members to identify the need for access to Users; obtain authority via Module Manager and User Management; control and monitor user access by Project Team.
	Supervise technical staff and control the delivery of Stage Products.
Skills Profile	Understanding of project management methods in use to plan and control the activities of Team Members under the direction of the Module Manager.
	Understanding of IT concepts and practices together with in-depth experience of the techniques and procedures used during Logical Design.
	Ability to conduct technical meetings and deliver presentations to both technical and user staff.
	Ability to identify training needs and to provide ad-hoc training to Team Members.
	High level analysis skills particularly in information gathering and inter-personal communication.
Training and Development	Training in management skills with emphasis placed on planning and estimating, staff motivation and presentation skills.
	Understand the aims and objectives of the user organisation and the systems that implement the business procedures.
	Track new developments in IT including hardware, software, development tools and methods. Developments which impact the analysis and design processes should be identified and evaluated.

Logical System Specification Process Modeller

Objectives
: To specify in detail the logical database update and enquiry processing which is implicit in the Requirements Specification.

  To define the interaction between users and the computer system by specifying the structure and navigation facilities of each dialogue identified in the Requirement Specification.

  To define the mechanisms by which users gain access to the dialogues they are authorised to execute.

  To document the products of Logical Design in accordance with the standards set by SSADM and the Module Manager.

Job Description
: Perform as many of the following tasks as directed under the supervision of the Team Leader.

  Define the structure, navigation and help facilities for each dialogue identified in the Requirements Specification.

  Define a menu hierarchy for each user role, which gives access to the dialogues allocated to the role.

  Update the ELHs with state indicator values and document the meaning of the values in the Entity Descriptions.

  Produce Update Process Models (UPM) and Enquiry Process Models (EPMs) as required.

Skills Profile	In-depth knowledge and experience of the logical design techniques namely dialogue design, entity - event modelling and logical database process design.
	Conversant with Data Dictionary concepts and familiarity with any CASE tool designated to document the Logical Design.
	General analysis/design skills and awareness of the concepts and good practices associated with Human Computer Interface design.
	Ability to converse knowledgeably with other technical specialists, in particular the Human Factors Specialists.
Training and Development	Training in technical and leadership skills.
	Education and training, at an overview level, in the technical specialist roles involved in the development process.
	Understand the functions and policies of the organisation.
	Monitor new developments in systems analysis and design tools and methods.
	Presentation and communication skills training.

Logical System Specification Product Developer

Objectives
To assemble the output from activities during the Stage into a cohesive set of end-product documentation which comprises the Logical Design.

To ensure the documentation meets the quality criteria and standards in terms of structure and content which have been set for the project.

To receive, control and amend all interim documentation produced during the Stage.

Job Description
Set up and manage a repository for the products of the Stage and those carried forward from Stage 3 which adhere to the Configuration Management and Documentation standards adopted for the project.

Attend technical and quality reviews and ensure that products are of the required standard prior to acceptance into the repository.

Provide indexing and cross referencing as needed within and across products making up the documentation set.

Follow the direction of the Module Manager and produce the overview, summary and supporting documentation necessary to complete the documentation set.

Assemble the final documentation set from the repository at the end for review of the Stage. Update the document set with the results of the review.

Skills Profile	Knowledge and experience of the Requirements Specification and Logical Design techniques.
	Conversant with Data Dictionary concepts and familiarity with any CASE tool or Desk Top Publishing (DTP) package designated to be used on the project.
	Thorough understanding of the concepts and practices of Configuration Management and Document Control.
	Good skills in technical writing and document production.
Training and Development	Training in technical and leadership skills with emphasis placed on technical writing and presentation skills.
	Education and training, at an overview level, in the technical specialist roles involved in the development process.
	Training in the concepts and practices of document layout and production with working experience of the facilities offered by various Desk Top Publishing (DTP) packages.
	Monitor new developments in systems analysis and design tools and methods.

Human Factors Specialist

Objectives
To assist the Logical System Specification Process Modeller with the production of Dialogue Structures to meet the requirements of the user roles in terms of usability.

To receive input regarding the implications for user procedures and job design.

SSADM Knowledge Required
Working knowledge of dialogue design and function definition.

Good understanding of the activities required of the user before, during and after the execution of a dialogue.

Services Provided
During Step 510:

Advice to the Logical System Specification Process Modeller in the identification and sequencing of logical groupings of data items. Guidance in the amount of navigation and level of help facilities appropriate to a given dialogue.

Capacity Planner

Objectives
: To assist in the evaluation of the completed Logical Design by testing it against the objectives and constraints set for the system.

SSADM Knowledge Required
: Working knowledge of the products of Logical Design.

Services Provided
: During Step 540:

    Estimate of the data sizes and placement requirements together with processing load and timings for each Function Definition from the results of Capacity Workload Modelling.

    Assessment of the feasibility of the Service Level Requirements based on adherence to the design objectives and the selected Technical Environment.

SSADM Roles

Stage 6 Physical Design

Introduction

The Physical Design Module enables procedures to be developed which are specific to the implementation environment.

Logical design is converted into physical design using these procedures, including the specification of any detail dependent on the physical environment.

Stage Roles

The following matrix shows the roles required in Stage 6 and a page number reference to the detailed description.

SSADM V4 Module SSADM V4 Stage	RA 1	RA 2	RS 3	LS 4	LS 5	PD 6
<u>SSADM Management</u>						
Module Manager	10	26	44	58	80	92
Team Leader	12	28	46	62	82	94
<u>Team Members</u>						
PD Process Modeller					68	97
PD Data Modeller					70	99
PD Product Developer						101
<u>Expert Roles</u>						
Capacity Planner			55	76	89	103
Database Administrator				77		104

Module Manager

Objectives	To control the production and assembly of a Physical Design which contains all the information necessary to construct and introduce the new system.
	To supervise the production of a set of standards covering the physical data and processing elements of the system.
	To ensure that the products meet the standards set for quality, content and structure.
	To allocate resources to meet, within budget, the timescale allowed for the completion of the Stage.
Job Description	Ensure that the Physical Environment Specification received from the IT Service Provider/Supplier is adequate for the specification of standards and the production of Activity Descriptions.
	Define a Product Breakdown Structure specific to the implementation environment and specify Product Descriptions which meet the quality, content and structural standards of the installation. Produce Activity Descriptions to support development of the products.
	Produce detailed plans for this Module which incorporate all activities and dependencies necessary to create the products identified in the Product Breakdown Structure and any additional activities required during this Stage. Agree these plans with the project manager.
	Initiate the preparation of user, operations and training manuals.
	Agree the Physical Design Strategy with the Project Manager.
	Monitor progress and resource utilisation of Stage Teams. Contingency plans for any exceptional situation that may arise.

	Attend progress meetings and produce/present regular reports to the Project Manager in accordance with the project management standards.
	Liaise with Project Manager and Team Leader(s) to identify the need for access to Users; obtain authority via Project Manager and User Management; control and monitor user access by Project Team.
Skills Profile	Experience of managing technical staff and delivering significant project products, especially Physical Design.
	Thorough understanding of a product based management method (preferably PRINCE) and sufficient working knowledge of SSADM to estimate effort and plan the Stage within the confines of the Module Plan.
	Technical experience of a general nature to allow full communication with Team Leaders, their teams and technical specialists.
	Imagination and skill in staff management, motivation and career development.
	Technical and business skills to take an active part in strategy decisions made during the Stage.
	High level analysis skills particularly in information gathering and inter-personal communication.
Training and Development	Continuing training in project management with emphasis placed on planning skills, staff selection and financial management.
	Broad management and business training to establish a better understanding of the organisation and the environment of senior user management.
	Monitor new developments in hardware, software, development tools and methods.
	Presentation and communication skills training.

Team Leader

Objectives
: To supervise the production of one or more components of the Physical Design as agreed with the Module Manager.

  To ensure that the products meet the standards set by the Module Manager for quality, content and structure.

  To ensure that the activities assigned are completed within the timescale and resource allocation stated in the Stage Plans. To report progress and status to the Module Manager.

Job Description
: Produce detailed Team Member work plans for the production of the components assigned by the Module Manager. Ensure that the activities and resources allocated are in accordance with the Stage Plans.

  Supervise the team in the production of the Application Development Standards and Implementation Strategy.

  Oversee the classification of the implementation environment and the development of DBMS and processing standards. Ensure that supporting design documentation is produced.

  Schedule and conduct technical reviews of all assigned products and sub-products. Schedule and conduct progress meetings with all Team Members and produce/present progress and exception reports to the Module Manager as directed.

  Liaise with other Team Leaders to ensure the consistency and coherence of products across teams. Arrange cross team reviews where necessary. Advise, guide and assist Team Members in production and the use of techniques and standards. Ensure that the standards, procedures and methods used were determined by the Module Manager.

  Ensure that all products and sub-products are of adequate standard for submission to a quality review.

Liaise with Module Manager, other Team Leader and own Team Members to identify the need for access to Users; obtain authority via Module Manager and User Management; control and monitor user access by Project Team.

Supervise technical staff and control the delivery of Stage Products.

Skills Profile

Understanding of project management methods in use to plan and control the activities of Team Members under the direction of the Module Manager.

Experience of managing technical staff and delivering significant project products, especially Physical Design.

Ability to conduct technical meetings with both technical and user staff.

Ability to communicate at a knowledgeable level with technical specialists.

Understanding of IT concepts and practices together with in-depth experience of the techniques and procedures used within SSADM during Physical Design.

Ability to identify training needs and to provide ad-hoc training to Team Members.

Display high level analysis skills particularly in information gathering and inter-personal communication.

SSADM Roles

Training and Development — Training in management skills with emphasis placed on planning and estimating, staff motivation and presentation skills.

Education and training, at an overview level, in the technical specialist roles involved in the development process.

Understand the user organisation, its aims and objectives and the systems that implement the business procedures.

Monitor new developments in IT including hardware, software, development tools and methods. Developments which impact the analysis and design processes should be identified and evaluated.

Physical Design Process Modeller

Objectives	To specify the components of functions not included in the Logical Design.
	To develop the Function Component Implementation Map to meet the requirements for quality, content and structure as stated in the Application Development Standards.
Job Description	Classify the processing implementation environment and develop the standards for the use of the physical processing system under the supervision of the Team Leader. Specify the naming standards for the application.
	Specify the implementation environment components for each function. Describe those components that can be specified non-procedurally to the physical processing system.
	Specify and design each procedural function component to a level of detail necessary for a programmer to implement.
	Provide advice and guidance to the Database Administrator in the task of developing a Process Data Interface.
Skills Profile	Knowledge and experience of the function definition and physical process specification techniques and experience of hardware and software characteristics of the implementation environment.
	Ability to converse knowledgeably with other technical specialists.

SSADM Roles

Training and Development Training in technical and leadership skills.

Education and training, at an overview level, in the technical specialist roles involved in the development process. Special attention to be paid to Database Administration and Capacity Planning.

Specific training in the concepts and use of products which make up the technical architectures within the organisation. This includes databases, application generators, software utilities, local and wide area networks and system management tools.

Understand the functions and policies of the organisation.

Monitor new developments in analysis and design tools and methods.

Presentation and communication skills training.

Physical Design Data Modeller

Objectives	To develop a Physical Data Design which implements the Required System Logical Data Model on the target DBMS and satisfies the objectives set for space utilisation and timing.
	To document the Physical Data Design to meet the requirements for quality, content and structure as stated in the Application Development Standards.
Job Description	Produce the DBMS Data Storage and Performance Classifications under the supervision of the Team Leader. Design the DBMS space and timing estimation forms. Specify the product data design rules.
	Produce a first-cut Physical Data Design which adheres to the standards set for the use of DBMS facilities using the product specific data design rules.
	Optimise the Physical Data Design to meet the objectives set for space utilisation and timings.
	Provide advice and guidance to the Database Administrator in the task of developing a Process Data Interface.
Skills Profile	Knowledge and experience of the logical data modelling and physical data design techniques together with experience of the hardware and software characteristics of the implementation environment.
	Ability to converse knowledgeably with other technical specialists.

Training and Development	Training in technical and leadership skills.

Education and training, at an overview level, in the technical specialist roles involved in the development process. Special attention to be paid to Database Administration and Capacity Planning.

Specific training in the concepts and use of products which make up the technical architectures within the organisation. This includes databases, application generators, software utilities, local and wide area networks and system management tools.

Understand the functions and policies of the organisation.

Monitor new developments in analysis and design tools and methods.

Presentation and communication skills training.

Physical Design Product Developer

Objectives
: To document and publish the Physical Design.

  To ensure that the documentation meets the quality criteria and standards in terms of the structure and content set for the project.

  To receive, control and amend all interim documentation produced during the Stage.

Job Description
: Set up and manage a repository, which adheres to the Configuration Management and Documentation standards adopted for the project, for the products of the Stage.

  Attend technical and quality reviews and ensure that products are of the required standard prior to acceptance into the repository.

  Provide indexing and cross referencing as necessary both within and across products making up the documentation set.

  Assist the Team Leaders and Team members in maintaining the Requirements Catalogue.

  Produce the overview, summary and supporting documentation to complete the documentation set under the direction of the Module Manager.

  Assemble the final documentation set from the repository for review at the end of the Stage. Update the document set as necessary with the results of the review and publish the Physical Design.

Skills Profile	Knowledge and experience of all techniques and concepts through to the end of Stage 6.
	Thorough understanding of the concepts and practices of Configuration Management and document control.
	Ability to communicate with other technical specialists and produce documentation which reflects the advice given.
	Practised in the use of any data dictionary or automated library facilities in use on the project.
	Good skills in technical writing and document production.
Training and Development	Training in technical and leadership skills with emphasis placed on configuration management and document control skills.
	Education and training, at an overview level, in all technical specialist roles involved in the development process.
	Training in the concepts and practices of document layout and production.
	Monitor advances in development environments and case tools, particularly libraries and dictionaries.
	Presentation and communication skills training.

Capacity Planner

Objectives	To assist in the creation of performance predictions and data storage requirements.
	To determine the capacity requirements of the new system.
SSADM Knowledge Required	Working knowledge of the concepts and products of Physical Design.
Services Provided	During Step 640:
	Help and assistance in the optimisation of the Physical Data Design by providing information generated from Workload Models.

Database Administrator

Objectives	To complete and validate the procedural specification and non-procedural implementation of the mapping between the physical data design and the logical view of the data.
	To provide expert knowledge and advice on the target implementation environment.
SSADM Knowledge Required	Working knowledge of physical process specification, physical data design and logical data modelling.
Services Provided	During Step 660:
	Production of the consolidated Process Data Interface with the assistance of the Physical Design Data and Process Modellers.

Bibliography

Information Systems Engineering Library

The Information Systems Engineering Library is published by CCTA and is available from HMSO Publications Centre, PO Box 276, London SW8 5DT.

The following module is referenced in this publication:

Interfacing SSADM and PRINCE
(due 1993)

Information Systems Guides

The Information Systems Guides, published by CCTA, are available from John Wiley & Sons Ltd, Baffins Lane, Chichester PO19 1UD.

The following guide is referenced in this publication:

IS Guide B Set: Systems Development Set
ISBN   0 471 92526 8
           0 471 92527 6
           0 471 92528 4
           0 471 92529 2
           0 471 92530 6
           0 471 92531 4
           0 471 92532 2
           0 471 92533 0

SSADM Documentation

The SSADM Version 4 Reference Manual is published by NCC Blackwell Ltd and is available from NCC Blackwell Ltd, 108 Cowley Road, Oxford, OX4 1JF.
ISBN 1 85554 004 5.

User Interface Guides

The User Information Guides, published by CCTA, are available from HMSO Publications Centre, PO Box 276, London SW8 5DT.

The following guides are referenced in this publication:

User Interface: The Issues
ISBN   0 946683 36 0

User Interface: Style Guide Issues
ISBN   0 946683 54 9

Glossary

	Definition of terms specific to SSADM are contained in the SSADM Version 4 Reference Manual.
CASE tool	Computer Aided Software Engineering (CASE) tool which supports the application of development techniques during SSADM modules, e.g. Logical Data Modelling or Data Flow Diagramming. Most CASE tools provide an integrated repository which holds the information recorded on the objects, e.g. entities, and normally provides facilities for reporting on the information and providing integrity checks.
Database Management System (DBMS)	A system that enables the definition and maintenance of physical databases and provides facilities for application processes to access the data. The data is organised in a logical manner to facilitate access by the applications. The precise organisation varies according to the database architecture supported, i.e. hierarchical, network or relational.
Data Dictionary	A computer database which contains the definition of system objects and includes accessing facilities to its definitions. The definitions may include logical definitions, e.g. entities and attributes, and physical definitions, e.g. databases, files and records. The dictionary may also include process definitions at logical and physical levels and other objects such as screen definitions. Some dictionaries contain links between these links. Data dictionaries may be associated with either DBMS or CASE tools.
DTP	Desk Top Publishing.

information management	The means by which an organisation maximises the efficiency with which it plans, collects, organises, uses, controls, disseminates and disposes of its information, and by which it ensures that the value and potential value of that information is identified and exploited to the fullest extent.
information system	Any procedure or process with or without IT support which provides a way of acquiring, storing, processing or disseminating information. Information systems include applications and their supporting infrastructure component.
IT Service Provider	The source, either internal or external to the organisation, which provides the IT services to perform the business of the organisation.
Logical System Specification Module (LS)	The objective is to produce the Logical System Specification. The Selected Technical System Option and the Technical Environment Description define the scope of the physical implementation. This detail must be consistent with the Logical Design.
Module Manager	A Module Manager is assigned, for each SSADM Module, with the responsibility for ensuring that the module products are produced on schedule, to agreed quality standards and within budget. The Module Manager is supported by Module Teams responsible for conducting the activities and producing the products of the Module.
Physical Design Module (PD)	The objective is to produce the Physical Design for the system based on the Logical System Specification and the Physical Environment Specification, i.e. it is implementation dependent.
PRINCE	PRojects IN Controlled Environments is a government developed methodology for project management with particular application to the management of Information Systems projects. It is a development of the PROMPT methodology which has been in use in government departments since 1983.

product

A product may be an item of software, hardware, documentation or a collection of other products. Each product is defined and its production planned within the project. Within the Product Breakdown Structure, there is a distinction between Management Products, Technical Products and Quality Products:

Management Products are produced as part of the management of the project. Technical Products are products which make up the system and Quality Products are produced for or by the quality process.

Product Breakdown Structure

Identifies the products which are required and must be produced by a project. This document describes the system in a hierarchical manner, breaking it down through a number of levels to the components of each product.

project

A project has the following characteristics:

- a defined and unique set of technical products to meet the business needs

- a corresponding set of activities to construct those products

- a certain amount of resources

- a finite lifespan

- an organisational structure with defined responsibilities.

Project Board

The Project Board is appointed by the IT Executive Committee or, possibly, the IS Steering Committee from where it derives its authority. It represents, at senior management level, the business, financial and technical interests of the organisation associated with a particular project. It approves, reviews and authorises the organisation, plans and resources for the project.

SSADM Roles

Project Manager — Appointed by the Project Board to assume day-to-day responsibility for management of the project through all its stages. Separating the general management responsibilities, i.e. the project manager, from the technical responsibilities, i.e. the stage manager, allows these roles to be assigned to the individuals with the most appropriate skills and experience.

Requirements Analysis Module (RA) — The objective is to produce the Analysis or requirements. Within this, the Selected Business Option defines the scope for further investigation.

Requirements Specification Module (RS) — The objective is to produce the Requirements Specification.

role — The various management and technical responsibilities within SSADM are assigned to a number of designated roles. These roles are assigned to individual people according to the needs of the project and the mix of skills available.

service — A set of related functions provided by an IT system which is seen and operated by users as a coherent and self-contained entity. A service may range from access to a single application program to the use of one or more global facility e.g. a transaction processing system, a suite of batch programs or a print system.

Team Leader — Responsible for managing a Stage team which may be created during a project. In certain circumstances team leaders are not appointed, in which case the Stage Manager assumes the responsibility of the team leader(s).

Index

Capacity Planner	55, 76, 89, 103
Corporate Security Specialist	23, 42, 56
Data Administrator	22, 54
Data Communications	78
Database Administrator	77, 104
Human Factors Specialist	41, 75, 88
IT Service Provider	38, 72
Logical System Specification Process Modeller	84
Logical System Specification Product Developer	66, 86
Module Manager	10, 26, 44, 58, 80, 92
Physical Design Data Modeller	70, 99
Physical Design Process Modeller	68, 97
Physical Design Product Developer	101
Requirements Analysis Data Modeller	16, 32
Requirements Analysis Process Modeller	18, 34
Requirements Analysis Product Developer	20, 36
Requirements Specification Data Modeller	48
Requirements Specification Process Modeller	50
Requirements Specification Product Developer	52
Senior Requirements Analyst	14, 30, 64
Staff Representative	39, 73
Systems Architect	40, 74
Team Leader	12, 28, 46, 62, 82, 94

SSADM Roles